# Manifesto
## of the
# Gifted Girl

### JOAN FRANKLIN SMUTNY

**Royal Fireworks Press**
Unionville, New York

# Introduction

The *Manifesto of the Gifted Girl* reaches out to girls and women in all walks of life and in every kind of circumstance. It strengthens, inspires, and counsels those who are struggling to find their place in school and society, as well as those who are launching out on their own for the first time. Framed with the voices of the girls themselves, the book is conversational and simply written so that both girls and young women, together with their advocates—parents, older friends, mentors—can gain strength and hope from the messages contained in its pages.

The *Manifesto* celebrates the gifts, hopes, and dreams of girls and guides them as they take their first steps into the larger world before them. Encompassing the academic, creative, and social-emotional domains of a gifted girl's life, the text includes three parts. The first two are: I. Who I Am; and II. What I Need. These sections focus on specific characteristics and needs expressed in the words of gifted girls and young women. The format begins with a quote from a girl and concludes with a one-paragraph response, providing guidance and counsel in specific areas of her life.

The last part—III. What I Can Do: My Vision for the Future—is a distillation of the dreams, hopes, and aspirations of gifted girls in many different communities. Each page begins with a girl's statement of what she can be, followed by a quote from a famous pioneer woman. It then concludes with a one-paragraph summary of this woman's achievement in a particular area of human endeavor.

It is my hope that this publication will aid gifted girls in honing the life skills they need to define themselves, find their own path into the future, and defend their fondest hopes from the sabotaging influences that too often hijack the lives of promising young women. For advocates of gifted girls, the Manifesto is a catalyst for discussion and reflection, and, hopefully, a call to action as well.

Royal Fireworks Press
41 First Avenue, PO Box 399
Unionville, NY 10988-0399
(845) 726-4444
FAX: (845) 726-3824
email: mail@rfwp.com
website: rfwp.com

ISBN: 978-0-89824-364-2

Printed and bound in the United States of America using vegetable-based inks on acid-free, recycled paper and environmentally-friendly cover coatings by the Royal Fireworks Printing Co. of Unionville, New York.

# I. Who I Am:

*I am good at many things and am ready to do more.*

You may not notice me, but look at what I do. I learn fast, and I'm always curious about what else there is to learn. I like to read and talk and ask questions—all the time! Sometimes I'm shy, but you'll still find me looking things up, checking the Internet, the library, and peering through my binoculars. A lot of things I try to do come easily, so I always want to learn more! When a teacher gives an assignment, I already have many ideas about how I want to do it. I wake up excited about all the things I want to do.

There's nothing wrong with girls and women admitting they are good at something. Everyone has special gifts, dreams, and hopes. If you put yourself down, you will lead a small life. Look at Toni Morrison, the first African American woman to win the Nobel Prize in literature. What if she said, "You know I'm really nothing much, just a little woman. I'll just hide here under a bush." Your intelligence is your strength but if you pretend you don't have it, then it might as well not exist. Claim it! Be it!

*I live all over the world, belong to every culture and speak every language, but I am still the one with the fire in her eyes.*

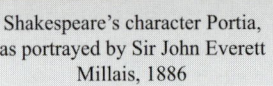

Sometimes I feel like everyone wants me to shut up and listen. Sometimes I wonder why I can't be excited and loud and jump around like my brothers. Sometimes it's easier to pretend to be the good girl, quiet and neat, who hardly ever speaks and never shouts. But watch out! There is a fire in my eyes. I am looking for an escape, and I will find it some day. I may be in a place where women have no rights, or I may be in a place where they do. But I will break out of my shell one day, you watch. I am the one with the fire in her eyes.

Shakespeare's character Portia, as portrayed by Sir John Everett Millais, 1886

Gifted girls and women don't look a certain way or live a certain life. Some live in societies where women have little freedom to make their own choices in life; others have more choices but get little guidance or encouragement to live larger lives. Like many of these girls and women, you may feel an eagerness to peck open your shell. You may hide this burning fire inside yourself because you don't want to get in trouble or be ridiculed. But remember that you must hold onto this dream and never let it go. You have a right to it no matter where you live, what language you speak, or how much money you have. Keep your eyes open, tell your dreams to someone who will listen, and let these dreams lead you to your path.

---

I don't always like adults helping me. Even if it would be easier for me just to listen and follow their directions, that's so boring! Just give me a hint or explain why my idea may not work, and then let me go on trying. Can't you see? I don't like to be told how to do things all the time. It makes me feel as if no one wants to hear what I have to say. And guess what? Even if I follow directions, I still may end up finding my own solution anyway, and that's the greatest feeling.

Detail of Madame Ginoux with Books, by Vincent Van Gogh, November, 1888 (or May, 1889?)

Girls and women don't have to be helpless and always look to an adult or a man to solve their problems. If you believe many of the television shows, movies, and other media, girls can't do anything for themselves! Yet, you are smart and can solve problems. In fact, you love to solve problems. So, before you run to someone else because you think you don't know what to do, find your own solutions. Use your mind. Some of the best inventions have come from problems that someone decided to solve in a new way. Be a problem solver! Don't hold back because you're afraid your solutions won't work. Step out and take a risk. Be bold. Solve a problem.

---

*I am full of surprises because I may not show the creative talents I have or share my imagination as I'd like to.*

---

I don't like following one track or being one thing. Why does everyone say I have to choose? My Dad says I should go for science and math, not creative writing because there's no real work for creative writers. A kid at school was surprised that I published a story in an online magazine because I'm so into science. Why can't I be creative and imaginative and also love science? Why do I have to give up some parts of myself for other parts? I like to think outside the box, so why should I live inside the box? I imagine stories whether or not I want to. And I write down stories people tell me in my neighborhood, and sometimes I hear poetry in my dreams.

One of the challenges gifted women have, especially in the pure science or math fields, is finding a way to include other talents and interests. Don't bar yourself from using and exploring your other passions in life because someone said they're not "practical" or don't relate to your primary interest. If you are creative, there are many ways to use imagination and creative reasoning in any subject. Don't shut the door on anything—you never know when some talent of yours will become important in the future. Your happiness comes from doing what you love and from living close to your heart, not from following what the world says you're "supposed to do."

*I am different from a lot of girls, but I still want to feel part of a community.*

I usually am alone. I am the girl who won't play the games many girls and women play. I won't pretend that I'm nobody, that my ideas don't matter. I won't speak like a second-class citizen, as if I need permission to voice an opinion. I can be bold, and this makes some girls laugh behind my back. The boys stare at me like a specimen from science class. Once in a while, I meet other girls who don't want to shut up and fold their hands. When I'm with like-minded friends, girls with many ideas, girls who won't let you get a word in edgewise because they have so much to say and they talk a mile a minute, I am happy.

Gifted girls and women want to feel the freedom to be themselves. But no one wants to be alone—the girl who can't fit in with anyone. Instead of trying to be like other girls, look for a kindred spirit. Being with others like you will help you feel that it's ok to dream big. If you cannot find anyone like you, then turn to the girls and women who've gone before you— the pioneers, painters, scientists. Put pictures of them on your walls. Their company can help you find what you love and take the first steps toward your own path in life. Pablita Velarde, a painter, once said that another painter, Tonita Pena, gave her "the inner strength that I needed to dare the men to put me in my own place or let me go."

I care about a lot of things in my school, community, and the world. I care about people, animals, nature, and justice. Things I would like to get rid of: bullying of unpopular kids, cruelty to animals, starvation of people living in drought, homelessness in my city. I have ideas on how we could make these problems better. I sometimes write speeches and imagine giving them to politicians or sending them to newspapers. Would anyone listen? I don't learn much about women philanthropists, inventors, or scientists in school. I know about Albert Einstein, but not as much about Marie Curie. Last year, we studied the work of Louis Leakey but what about Jane Goodall or Diane Fossey?

Gifted girls and women are drawn to issues in their environment as well as in the larger world around them. Even though they have more freedoms today than they had in the past, many still hesitate to debate or speak up when they don't agree with a teacher or a male peer. The courage to speak up is important. If you and other girls like you stay silent, then half of the world's population has no voice! If you have strong views about some issue in your community, your school, or your country, find ways to express them. Refuse to be silent. You have every right to care about what happens around you and to express your own ideas, whether you do it through words, art, or action.

*I know I am beautiful, inside and out and don't need other people to define me.*

When my mother says I'm beautiful, I smile. Others have a different perspective. Walking down the hall, I feel the eyes of the other kids on my clothes, my hair, my shoes. They aren't as nice as my mom. I know that looks are important in this world, and I try to look my best. A smile is the most important part of my looks, and I wear it everywhere. It says that I am beautiful on the inside where it really counts, and I work harder on that than on my nails.

Marie-Elisabeth Cavé, aged 24, by Auguste-Dominique Ingres.

Gifted girls and women care as much about beauty as do others. This is normal, but they shouldn't feel pressured to define themselves by what others say is beautiful. Your outer beauty extends from the beauty you hold within you. You can take steps to care for your appearance—discovering new styles of clothing, exploring different applications for hair, skin, or nails. You can do this without becoming trapped by the beauty game that the media plays. You are not a piece of meat, or an object for other people to pass judgment on. You should love expressing beauty, but it should also extend to the inner life of your soul—how you treat others, what you value, and how you express yourself.

Roman marble statue of the first century AD; copy of a Greek bronze statue of about 460 BC

I want to pursue the sports I enjoy, and I want to develop my athletic skills. Being slim and fit is part of looking good and being healthy. As I grow up, I need activities that I enjoy and that will keep me in shape. Team sports give me a chance to work on athletic skills with other kids; we all have to work together to win as a team, and I use my skills to get every-one to cooperate for the same goal.

Gifted girls enjoy the comradeship of sports, provided the sport is one they excel in and one that challenges them both physically and mentally. Don't turn your back on this possibility because someone tells you that you're not the "athletic type." Athletics can give you a place where you can express your strength and leadership without having to hold back. The team structure also allows you to share leadership and help to create a healthy sense of community. It's im-portant for you to pursue athletic interests and not feel that your academic abilities limit you to intellectual things. Athleticism suited to your needs and interests can increase your strength and give you a body image beyond the traditional feminine one.

Little Dancer Aged Fourteen, by Edgar Degas

My relationships are important to me, but sometimes I feel torn between my family and my friends. I don't like to trash my family the way some of my friends do because I know my family loves me and how hard they try. But I also want to spend more time with my friends because they give me things that my family can't. I feel different with them. Sometimes my family wants to know everything I'm doing—like I'm four years old—and that makes me want to run out the door. So I try to remember everything my family's done for me and where my roots are. But I also have to stretch out and reach for the skies, and that means friends and new people.

Because of their unique abilities and needs, many gifted girls have strong relationships with their families or other adults. When you see how your family members, or relatives, or teachers support your abilities, stick up for you when you need it, and help you find outlets for your talents and interests, it's good to be grateful. But it's also normal to value your friendships (with girls or boys), particularly when you feel misunderstood or alone. As you move into adulthood, you will need the support of caring adults *and* friends. The first provides roots for your growth. The second gives you a place in the world outside your doors—a community with whom you can share your values, goals, and dreams.

> *I can't help feeling the needs of those around me and doing what I can to make their lives better.*

---

**I feel others' feelings so much that I'm sometimes overwhelmed.** When my uncle stayed with us, I could feel his sadness about losing his job, and when he took me to the museum, I could tell he was just pretending to be ok. I wish I wasn't so sensitive to everything that lives! A cat yowls outside, and I stay awake worrying about it. A kid at school gets teased, and I want to karate chop the guy who sneered at him. Sometimes I help animals before I even know what I'm doing. My Mom will say, "What are you doing with that blanket?" But she knows I'm putting it in a box outside for the homeless cat. People think I go too far, but they don't lie in bed at night imagining how it would feel to wander around the streets with no warm place to curl up in.

Gifted girls need support in managing their sensitivity for the feelings of others. They want to make a difference—to know what steps they can take to improve their lives. You need to see that your sensitivity toward others is a strength, not a weakness or vulnerability. Examples abound of women whose keen response to the plight of others enabled them to accomplish great things in the world. Eleanor Roosevelt, Harriet Tubman, Susan B. Anthony, and many others stepped boldly onto the world stage and risked their own safety because they cared for their fellow beings and wanted to do what they could to rectify wrongs. Part of making a difference in the lives of others is knowing when and how to act. Sometimes, other people may rely on you too much and make you feel pressured to help with every problem. You can give your light, but don't give away your oil.

# II.   *What I Need*

*I can't succeed alone. I need the support of my parents and teachers to make the most of my gifts.*

The school I go to is like a box. All I care about is getting out of here some day. Every year, I think, ok, how many years before I apply to college? But I don't know if my good grades in here will help me out there. What if I apply and can't do the tests because I never learned the math or history or whatever I need to get in? The school counselor says I can go far because I'm smart. But then my mom says I should get nurse's training because they always need nurses and at least I could get a job. That just kills my spirit when she says that. I nod and say, yeah Mom, but it kills me inside. Because that's just not what I want for my life, ever!

Gifted girls may be created equal, but not all have the support and education they need to realize their talents. Yet, there are ways for promising girls like you to move ahead. Ask your parents, counselors, and teachers to help you find resources. There are organizations and funding sources that seek talent all over the country. Universities know that students like you need support, especially if your school didn't give you all the skills and knowledge you need to apply to the universities of your choice. Don't think that because you're in a neighborhood with few resources, that you're stuck. Talk to your teachers, your relatives, your library, your community center. When you show the world how serious you are, helpers may appear where you least expect.

I love being around smart girls who want to do a lot of different things. I love it when I don't have to feel weird because I'm into art or a book I'm reading. Instead, these girls just say, "What's that you're doing?" And I feel like they're really interested. I like girls who won't be anyone's stereotype—girls who are pretty, but also strong and smart. You can be smart and not this geeky girl with weird clothes who's just clueless. I learned from being with other girls in a special math program that you don't have to be defined by your abilities. You can be really good at something and still hang out with your friends and see a movie.

Detail of Woman Reading in a Landscape, by Jean-Baptiste-Camille Corot

Gifted girls who spend time together discover that they're not alone. This is a powerful lesson in itself and immediately helps to free them from the idea that something's wrong with them. It's important that you not doubt yourself because you feel different from other kids your age. After a while, you may start to hide your gifts and pretend to be "like everyone else," and this will lead you to express yourself less and less. If you need help finding other girls like you, talk to your family or adults at school (a teacher, counselor, coach). Explore different places: a gifted program, an art class, an ecology class, an online community. Search the internet and apply for an institute that supports talented, motivated girls. This will help you feel normal *as yourself.* And the more normal you feel, the easier it will be for you socially.

*I need a classroom that's less about competition and more about everyone doing her best.*

---

When someone wins, someone else loses. In a spelling bee, everyone is tense. No one breathes because at any moment, you could slip and fall. When someone does, you hear the sigh in the room and the kid walking off the platform pretending not to care. I won the bee and wish I hadn't. To me it's a game and should be fun, like when I play checkers with my sister. But now I'm the girl who won the bee. Can't I just be the girl who did better than she ever did before? If I could be anything, it wouldn't be "the best this" or "the best that," but it would be the girl who invented something wonderful or traveled to a far corner of the earth on foot.

Gifted girls enjoy competition in the spirit of fun or as a way to test their own limits. You're not alone if your sensitivity for the feelings of others makes you feel uncomfortable "beating" fellow students in a competition or game. You may love the thrill of winning and receiving awards but you don't want others to ridicule you or treat you as if you're above them. It's normal for you to be happy when you do well or when you help your winning team. With practice, you can find a balance between celebration and sensitivity toward others. The ideal classroom for you is one that focuses less on who's the best, the fastest, the smartest. If you're in a class that gets too competitive, step back. Free yourself to play your own game—which is to do your best.

*I need to be creative in my studies at least some of the time and to be free to do things in a different way.*

---

I see many ways to go where some people see just one. I imagine many worlds even though people say the one we live in is all there is. Did you know that birds see more color than we do? I am like the bird. I can't help what I see. A teacher will tell us, this is how you do it. Can I keep myself to the one way? I feel as if I have a little elf in my mind, one who doesn't like it and it's all I can do to make her behave! She whispers in my ear, try this, try that, and I can't say no all the time. So I wonder, can I try a different way at least some of the time?

Creativity is an important part of learning for girls like you. It allows you to make discoveries. Look for the creative dimension in all subjects (using the visual arts, performing arts, and creative thinking programs). Through creativity, you can explore, invent, and imagine. The opportunity to step away from high-pressured academics to express your individual vision and ideas allows you to step away from the cycle of learning that you're used to. Creativity helps you connect to what you're studying—to put your own stamp on it!

*I need to learn more about the lives of girls and women of all cultures, countries, and times.*

---

An astronomer came to our school today. She was tall with long, black hair, and she told us stories from her life on the reservation. She came a long way, she said, from the days when she and her mother cleaned offices to make money. Someone asked what kept her going, how did she get to college and then to the field of astronomy? "Look where you want to go." That's what she said. "Look where you want to go. Too many people look at the things that scare them or that make them sad." I wrote that on my hand because I didn't bring a notebook. I want to be like her. When she left, everyone thought the same thing: A girl who grew up with nothing is now walking among the stars.

Gifted girls need to know more about women achievers—the pioneers, inventors, performers, artists, architects, astronauts, politicians, and athletes. Learning about their struggles, experiences, and triumphs will open up the world for you. Your curriculum should include more women of all backgrounds and explore their stories and achievements. Meeting women from different fields is also important and helps you see what it takes to endure hardship and persist through difficult times. Ask your teachers, your librarians, and your parents about great women. Their lives are maps to your own future.

My teacher asked me to direct a mural project, and I froze. Can I do this? Will anyone listen to what I have to say? My mother said, "Yes, of course. Don't worry. You are an artist; that's why the teacher asked you." Alone in my bed at night, the question looms: Can I do this? I who sit quietly at the back of the room because I don't want anyone checking me out? Is that a leader? I hope the teacher will help me. I hope she will show me how to guide the other students. I hope I know how to do it and that there's another way to lead besides boss, boss, boss. That's not my way. I still wonder, can I really do this?

Gifted girls need a chance to lead, but also guidance on how to do so. Leadership is a challenge, and part of the challenge for you must be to discover your own leadership style. There isn't just one way to be a leader. Gifted girls who are sensitive and intuitive are less likely to feel comfortable telling others what to do. Instead, you need to learn how to inspire others, help them commit to common goals, and guide them toward their achievement. Give yourself time to learn these skills, and ask for help. Adults—parents, teachers, neighbors—are there to empower you to find your own way of leading and can help you make the most of your strengths.

KEMMITZ

I'm at a fork in the road. Where do I go? Can I go back if the road is wrong? We had a career day at school and I, with my long list of things I love to do, went home as lost as before. If I take the left fork and go to a school that's best in the sciences, I'm afraid of what I'll leave behind: the poems I love writing, the modern dance classes I take three times a week. Will I lose all that? If, on the other hand, I choose the right fork and study literature, will I miss science? I'm at the fork in the road, wondering how to leave a part of myself on the road I don't take.

Woman in White, by Pablo Picasso

Gifted girls often struggle when they feel compelled to choose something that a parent, a teacher, or a friend believes is best. If you have multiple talents and interests, you need to find ways to make the most of all your strengths. Don't settle for less. Don't take "no" for an answer or believe that you can only do one thing. Tell those who love you that you're looking for something different. Look more deeply into subjects and fields you love, and see where your interests lead you. If you have a passion for both science and writing, for example, you will discover that in many science professions, you can do both; or in science journalism, if you choose that direction. Keep exploring the fields that call to you, asking questions and listening to your own heart.

I want to be an architect. I've known this for a long time. When I close my eyes, I see shapes and designs of different kinds of dwellings—a house built on the side of a cliff, a bungalow covered with solar panels that wraps around a hill. I imagine homes designed around nature with tree trunks in the middle of a living room. I work hard in math because I think I'll need that if I want to be an architect, and I do art too. I see the world in shapes and lines and angles and designs. I wish I knew a real architect who could show me what architects do every day. I would like to be a green architect and make solar homes that blend in with the land around them.

When a gifted girl has a strong interest in a subject or field not studied in school, a mentorship could be the answer. A mentor can guide your interest in a way most suited to your abilities and background, and can give you wise counsel on how to go forward. A good mentor feeds your imagination and hunger for knowledge but also opens a window to a world you may never have seen before. A mentor can tell you what the field is like for her—what she had to overcome, what she has been able to achieve.

Roman marble bust,
copy of earlier Greek statue

---

I keep my dreams in my heart. I live in a nice house in a nice neighborhood, where everyone does the same thing: college, good job, settle down in nice neighborhood. My mom says we should be grateful for what we have, and I am. But my dreams will always be different from this life. I dream of climbing Mt. Kiliminjaro. I dream of planting trees in South America. I dream of filming the Moon Bears in Southeast Asia. Not everyone understands these dreams, and some say ha ha ha, she's just kidding. My parents don't laugh, but I get the feeling that they think these dreams are just a phase. I hope not.

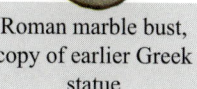

Gifted girls are dreamers. Full of enthusiasm, inspired by the possibilities of life, they imagine what they might become,

Roman marble bust, copy of earlier Greek statue

where they might go, and how they might get there. No matter how unusual, the dreams are yours. Your future is wide open, if you work hard and stay focused on your goals. The last thing anyone should do is tell you to lower your sights, to be "practical," to do the thing you most love as a "hobby." If you want more than anything to be an actress, try to be one! Find someone who will support your steps, share her wisdom and life experience, and then let you act on your deepest commitments. Remember that even if a door closes, you can find an opening somewhere else. Nothing is more important than the dreams of your heart.

---

Head of a Neapolitan Girl, 1881
Pierre-Auguste Renoir

I can't help caring what others hope and want for me. Sometimes, I give and give and give and bits of me start to disappear. I help with the other kids because Mom has to work. I help at the store. I help my grandmother with little chores. It's ok to help. But when they start saying, "Maybe you should go to college here in town or learn something more practical than history and art," I think, oh no. I will never go. More pieces of me will disappear until there is nothing left. I dream about a scholarship to go to a major university, and that is the future I want. I will work for it, study for it, plan for it, and I will make my life my own.

Gifted girls need adults who don't impose their own expectations on them. Be thankful for the people in your life who celebrate your successes, support your interests, and do not pressure you. You need a safe haven away from the pressures that make you feel they have no choices in life. You need caring guides who can respond to your unique qualities and remind you of them when you feel so pressured to achieve that you forget the important things: your larger goals in life, your friendships, your loved ones. Keep asking yourself, "Is this what I want?" Never set your own hopes and goals aside but look toward the far horizon—your deepest desire. Remind yourself every day, "this is my life."

# III.  What I Can Do:

## My Vision For The Future

I can be a trailblazer and discover things no one has known before.

Photo of Jane Goodall from 1964
Hugo van Lawick

**We have a choice to use the gift of our life to make the world a better place— or not to bother.**

*Jane Goodall*

Born in 1934, primatologist Jane Goodall's major breakthrough was the discovery of tool-making among chimpanzees. Though many animals had been clearly observed using "tools," previously only humans were thought to make tools, and tool-making was considered the defining difference between humans and other animals. This discovery convinced many scientists to reconsider their definition of being human.

Jane Goodall at Hong Kong University on 24 October 2004 with Mr. H

*I have the strength and agility to run, turn and leap in the air.*

---

When I'm skating, I feel like I can do anything. I feel like I can stay out there forever.

*Kristi Yamaguchi*

Born in 1971, figure skater, Kristi Yamaguchi became the first athlete of Asian descent to win the Olympic Gold medal in figure skating in 1992. She also won the Gold Medal in the World Figure Skating Championships in 1991 and 1992.

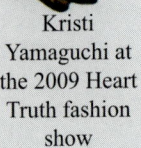

Kristi Yamaguchi at the 2009 Heart Truth fashion show

**The one thing I appreciated was the fact that when so many others, by the hundreds and by the thousands, joined in...I could feel that whatever my individual desires were to be free, I was not alone.**

*Rosa Parks*

Rosa Parks in 1955, with Martin Luther King, Jr. in the background

Born in 1913, Rosa Parks sent shockwaves through America when she refused to obey a bus driver and give up her seat for a white passenger. Her action sparked the Montgomery Bus Boycott in which thousands of African Americans refused to use the buses, choosing to walk many miles instead. Rosa Parks became an important symbol for a vision of equality among the races. The U.S. Congress later acknowledged her as the "Mother of the Modern-Day Civil Rights Movement."

*I can be nature's best friend by protecting her from those who want to exploit Her.*

**The planting of trees is the planting of ideas. By starting with the simple act of planting a tree, we give hope to ourselves and to future generations.**

*Wangari Maathai*

Wangari Maathai —photo by Martin Rowe

Born in Nyeri, Kenya, in 1940, Wangari Muta Maathai was the first woman in East and Central Africa to earn a doctorate degree. During the 1970s and 1980s, she launched a tree-planting initiative with local women's groups that quickly became a broad-based, grassroots organization designed to conserve the environment and improve the peoples' quality of life. Through her Green Belt Movement, she has assisted women in planting more than 20 million trees on their farms, schools, and church compounds. In 1986, the Movement spread beyond Kenya and included a Pan African Green Belt Network that continues today to spread to other African countries. Wangari Maathai is an internationally recognized champion for democracy, human rights, and environmental conservation. She and the Green Belt Movement have received numerous awards, most notably the 2004 Nobel Peace Prize.

*I can create things of such power and beauty that people will feel inspired.*

**The variation contained many low, fast jumps near the floor, lots of quick footwork, sudden changes of direction, off-balance turns, turns from** *pointe* **to** *pointe***, turned-in, turned-out positions, one after another. It was another way of moving...**

*Maria Tallchief*

Born in 1925, Maria Tallchief became one of the country's leading ballerinas from the 1940s to the 1960s. The daughter of an Osage tribe member, she was a trailblazer for Native Americans in the world of ballet. After joining the New York City Ballet, she became a popular figure in such works as *Orpheus, Miss Julie, Firebird,* and *The Nutcracker*, dazzling audiences with her extraordinary technique, musicality, and strength.

*I can investigate serious problems and report on them for all the world to see.*

Nellie Bly in 1890

**Could I pass a week in the insane ward at Blackwell's Island? I said I could and I would. And I did.**

*Nellie Bly*

Born in 1864, Nellie Bly became a celebrity when she had herself committed to an insane asylum to expose the conditions there as an undercover journalist for the *New York World*. Her work sparked reforms in the prison system. In 1890 she also embarked on a journey to travel around the world faster than Phileas Fogg in Jules Verne's novel, *Around the World in 80 Days*; she arrived in New York in 72 days, a world record at that time. Her book, *Around the World in 72 Days*, became a best seller.

**Humans are allergic to change. They love to say, "We've always done it that way." That's why I have a clock on my wall that runs counterclockwise.**

*Grace Hopper*

Commodore Grace M. Hopper,
USNR Official portrait
photograph

Born in 1906, Rear Admiral Grace Hopper was a pioneer Computer Programmer and devoted to the Navy. She changed the lives of everyone in the computer industry by developing the Bomarc system, later called CO-BOL (common-business-oriented language). COBOL made it possible for computers to respond to words rather than numbers. A true visionary who understood the role of developing computing languages to make computers user-friendly instruments throughout society, she became known as the Grand Lady of Software, Amazing Grace and Grandma COBOL.

Captain Grace M. Hopper, USNR
Working in her office, August 1976

*I can go into space and lead the way for girls who feel a kinship with the stars*

**My dream, now, is that people will discover and invent new ways to fly higher, faster, and farther ,and that someday humans will travel beyond our solar system.**

*Eileen Collins*

Eileen Collins, on October 30, 1998, posing for her official STS-93 portrait. She is wearing an orange Launch and Entry Suit, and is holding the helmet

Born in 1956, Eileen Collins has become a pioneer in the world of aviation. In February of 1995, after several years of training with NASA, she became the first female astronaut to pilot a space shuttle mission. She served as second-in-command of the shuttle *Discovery* during its rendezvous with the Russian space station Mir.

In recognition of her achievement as the first female Shuttle Pilot, she received the Harmon Trophy (an award for outstanding aviation).

Eileen Collins,
February 9, 1999

**Do the one thing you think you cannot do. Fail at it. Try again. Do better the second time. The only people who never tumble are those who never mount the high wire. This is your moment. Own it.**

*Oprah Winfrey*

Photo of Oprah Winfrey at her 50th birthday party at Hotel Bel Air - Alan Light, 2004

Born in 1954, Oprah Winfrey's broadcasting career began at age 17 when she was hired by WVOL radio in Nashville, and two years later signed on with WTVF-TV in Nashville as a reporter/anchor. She took over the reins of a faltering talk show in Chicago, which she then boosted to first place in 1985, renaming it "The Oprah Winfrey Show." In 1987, "The Oprah Winfrey Show" received three Daytime Emmy Awards. In 1988, Oprah Winfrey herself received the International Radio and Television Society's "Broadcaster of the Year" Award, the youngest person and only the fifth woman ever to receive the honor in IRTS's 25-year history.

*I can lead a people and give them a new vision of the future.*

Eleanor Roosevelt speaking at the
United Nations in July 1947

**You gain strength, courage, and confidence by every experience in which you really stop to look fear in the face.**

*Eleanor Roosevelt*

Although she had already won international respect and admiration in her role as First Lady to President Franklin D. Roosevelt from 1933 to 1945, Eleanor Roosevelt's work on the Universal Declaration of Human Rights would become her greatest legacy. This declaration was the first global expression of rights for all human beings. The delegates elected Eleanor Roosevelt to be their Chairperson. Like so many people throughout the world, the delegates recognized Eleanor Roosevelt's unparalleled humanitarian convictions, commanding leadership, and sharp intelligence.

Roosevelt and Fala, the
Roosevelts' dog during the
White House years